# THE
# AUTHOR
## IN YOU

{ A Handbook for Aspiring Authors }

### Kerri-Ann Haye-Donawa

## CONCLUSIO
HOUSE PUBLISHING

# THE
# AUTHOR
## IN YOU

{ A Handbook for Aspiring Authors }

Printed in Canada

First Printing, 2015

ISBN: 978-0-9949204-2-3

Published by:

**Conclusio House Publishing**
503-7700 Hurontario Street
Suite 209
Brampton, ON
L6Y 4M3

www.conclusiohouse.com

*"When asked, 'How do you write?' I invariably answer, 'One word at a time.'"*
~Stephen King

---

*"Start writing, no matter what. The water does not flow until the faucet is turned on."*
~Louis L'Amour

---

*"You only learn to be a better writer by actually writing."*
~Doris Lessing

# Acknowledgements

I extend deep gratitude to my dear friend, Nadia Brown, whose idea this was in the first place. Your help and support is invaluable, and I thank God for you more frequently than I let you in on. I'm not sure what I ever did to deserve you, but you've become more than a best friend to me. Love you, girl.

Thank you to the Conclusio House graphic design team—Naomi Fergusson and Mehala Hani—for helping me pull this little project together in an extremely short period of time. Your expertise and professionalism help make this company what it is.

And finally, thank you to my husband, parents, and siblings. Your support for me keeps me going, even when I'm out of breath.

# Table of Contents

Introduction                                      x

Chapter 1: What's in a Book?                      1

Chapter 2: Understanding Genre & Audience         5

Chapter 3: Improving Your Writing                 13

Chapter 4: Developing Your Idea into a Book       22

Chapter 5: Keys to Being a Successful Author      31

Chapter 6: Writing a Project Description          38

References                                        44

# Introduction

I t's a great time to write a book. Well, honestly, it's always a great time to write a book. But right now, at this particular moment in history, at this precise epoch in time, the stars are aligned, so to speak, for writers to succeed. The market is ripe, technological advances have set a stage quite easily mounted, and the gates to the publishing world are sprawling wide open.

If you've ever dreamt of becoming an author, or ever wished to share your thoughts with the world, you can now do so with relative ease. It's the wave that has stealthily crept onto the shores of the publishing landscape and has engulfed the sandcastles this industry has created over the past century. It's called self-publishing, and many have subscribed to its ease. There are many benefits to self-publishing, the most obvious one being the speed at which your manuscript becomes a book.

The following are some key differences between traditional publishing and self-publishing:

| Traditional Publishing | Self-Publishing |
| --- | --- |
| A publisher decides whether to accept or reject your manuscript | Author can publish manuscript at any time once complete |
| If publisher accepts the manuscript, they buy the rights to the book from the author | Author retains the rights to the book |
| Publisher is responsible for all expenses related to the production of the book | Author is responsible for all expenses related to the production of the book |
| Publisher controls the content and design of the book | Author controls the content and design of the book |
| Publisher responsible for the marketing, promotion, and distribution of the book | Author responsible for the marketing, promotion, and distribution of the book |
| Recoups their expenses before paying a percentage of the sales in royalties to the authors | Author benefits from all the profits of their sales. |

With the ease at which books can now be uploaded to the internet and shared with the world, there are new books being released every single day. But that doesn't mean that there isn't a market for all these books. In fact, every book has its select audience, and there's a big, wide world populated by billions of consumers who buy these special books every day. Nevertheless, a simple rule applies across the board—the better your book is, in terms of quality, content, presentation, and marketability, the more likely it is to do well.

I originally started writing this handbook for an author's workshop that I was facilitating. I wanted the aspiring authors who attended the workshop to leave with something tangible that they could use throughout their writing journey. Then I figured why not create something that all my clients could reference while writing their books. Consequentially, this handbook has been written with the aspiring author in mind. It provides an overview of the basic anatomy of a book, insight into genre and audience knowledge, tips on improving your writing and, by extension, your manuscript, as well as a step-by-step guide to developing your own idea into a marketable book. Use this handbook to steer the author in you in the right direction as you write and plan your career as an author.

Now, go write that book. Who knows? You may be the next best-selling author.

# CHAPTER 1

# What's in a Book?

E very book is different. Books differ in size, genre, appearance, design, even in feel and texture, but there are certain features that remain the same across the board, rudimentary building blocks that make a book a book. While not every element is essential, each is important and unique in the purpose it serves.

Here is the basic anatomy of a generic book:

➤ **Dedication:** *The Dedication is a part of the 'front matter' of a book. It comes after the title and copyright pages in a book. The Dedication is a personal note written by the author stating to whom the book is dedicated. It can range in length from a couple of words to multiple paragraphs. It is not an essential element, but is usually included in many kinds of books and adds a personal touch to the work.*

- ➢ **Acknowledgments:** *The Acknowledgments are also a part of the front matter of a book. As the name implies, the author uses the acknowledgements to thank those he/she feels indebted to in some way (for example, someone who was instrumental along his/her journey to becoming an author). This is not an essential element, but is usually included at the beginning of most books.*

- ➢ **Table of Contents:** *Unlike the Dedication and the Acknowledgments, this is an essential element to many kinds of books, with a few exceptions. Also a part of the front matter, the Table of Contents is the directory or map that guides readers to the contents of your book. It includes the chapter/parts/headings in a book along with their page numbers or location within the book.*

- ➢ **Foreword:** *The foreword is written by someone other than the author (never by the author herself). The person selected to write the foreword is usually accomplished in some way, either in the subject or industry about which the book is written or whose name is well known. The purpose of the foreword is to endorse the book or the author. The foreword writer may discuss* his relationship with the author or the value of the work in terms of its contribution to the field of study or literary scene. This is not an essential element.

➢ **Preface:** *The preface is a personal introduction to the book written by the author to her readers. In it the author tells the reader why she chose to write the book, what her inspiration or motivation was, what the book is about, the particulars of her process, and what she hopes to accomplish. This is not an essential element for all books, but works nicely for many non-fiction books.*

➢ **Introduction:** *Similar to a preface, but more of an overview of the book itself, the introduction states what it is about, why it is useful, and how it is to be used by the reader, amongst other things. It is not necessary to have both a preface and an introduction as the information may become redundant. Again, this is not an essential element, but it is an important element to many books, particularly non-fiction books.*

➢ **Body:** *The most essential part of every book is the meat of the book's content—the Body. The Body is made up of sections, chapters, headings, and everything the author has to say in between.*

*It makes up the bulk of the book. It is essentially why the reader purchased the book.*

➢ **Bibliography:** *The Bibliography is an important part of many non-fiction books. It lists the sources cited as well as the data essential to finding those sources (publisher, year published, edition, etc.)*

➢ **Index:** *This is an alphabetical list of names, topics, important words, and other specific information mentioned in the book along with the location indicators (page numbers).*

As stated above, not all these sections are essential to every book. In fact, if they are all included, the book would be rather crowded. Be sure to include the sections that are key to your particular genre, which we will discuss in the next chapter.

# CHAPTER 2

# Understanding Genre & Audience

K nowing and understanding your genre determines how you frame your book and the sections you include. The word *genre* simply means class or category. When it comes to literature, there are several main categories and smaller subcategories into which literary works can classified.

Below are a few of the genres as well as a small selection of the many subcategories that exist:

## Nonfiction

This is the category of literature that is based on true life events or information that is either factual or believed to be factual. The works in this category are usually made up of prose writing as opposed to poetry or script writing.

The subcategories within nonfiction are quite

extensive, which gives room for many different types of works. Here is a small selection of the categories available within this genre:

> **Biography & Autobiography** – *books written about the lives of others or oneself. Subtopics within this category include General [biographies], Personal Memoirs, Religious, Sports, Political, People with Disabilities, and many others.*

> **Education** – *books written for educational purposes; subtopics comprise Professional Development, Science, History, Leadership, Urban Studies, and many others.*

> **Self-Help** – *books written for personal growth or to help people overcome certain struggles and difficult issues. This category includes works on Aging, Grief, Abuse, Success, Fashion, Spiritual[ity], Body Image, to name a few.*

> **Family & Relationships** – *books written to help or support people in their family and personal relationships.*

*Subtopics within this category include Adoption & Fostering, Dating, Divorce & Separation, Friendship, Love & Romance, Marriage, Parenting, and more.*

➢ **Religion** – *books written on religious subject matter. Subtopics within this category include Biblical Studies, Christian Life, Christian Ministry, Christian Theology, and within these subtopics are even smaller topics, like women's issues, spiritual growth, spiritual warfare, prayer, devotional, family, and others. Within Religion are books written on any world religion.*

The nonfiction category is large and diverse. Therefore, any book that is written on a subject that is deemed real or factual will fall into a predetermined category. (See the Resources page at the back of the book.)

## Fiction

Works that originate from the imagination are considered fiction. This category of books comprises short stories, novels, and writings based on people or events that are fictitious (not real).

Like nonfiction, this category is made up several

subcategories to further classify the many different kinds of stories and works written as fiction. Below are a few of the many subcategories that exist, and the titles are quite self-explanatory.

- ➤ *Action & Adventure*
- ➤ *Historical*
- ➤ *Religious*
- ➤ *Erotica*
- ➤ *Black Humor*
- ➤ *Amish & Mennonite*
- ➤ *Christian*
    - − *Classic*
    - − *Romance*
    - − *Historical*
    - − *Fantasy*
    - − *Futuristic*
    - − *Suspense*
- ➤ *Crime*
- ➤ *Coming of Age*
- ➤ *Superheroes*
- ➤ *Thrillers*
- ➤ *Fairy Tales, Folk Tales, Legends & Mythology*

- Horror
- Medical
- Mystery & Detective
- Psychological
- Romance
  - Historical
  - Science Fiction
  - Time Travel
  - Paranormal

Fiction books can be as diverse as writers and readers. Therefore, like any good story, there are different themes that run throughout different books. See the Resource section on the last page of this book for a link to view the many categories and genres that have been established by the Book Industry Study Group.

## Poetry

The poetry genre is dedicated solely to poetic works. But like fiction and nonfiction, it hosts a range of classifying subheadings that group the different poetic creations published daily. The subheadings are largely geographic and cultural; for *example, African, Caribbean, Asian,* and *Middle Eastern.* However, there are also other classifiers like *Epic, LGBT,* and *Women Authors.*

# Juvenile Literature — Children & Young Adult

Children and Young Adult books are works written for a young audience. The classifiers within this genre are vast and as specific as the individual animal, country, or holiday being dealt with. A children's book can be classified as *Juvenile Fiction/Animal/Birds*, for example, or as *Juvenile Nonfiction/Animals/Foxes*, so it is important to know what specific category your book falls into. For the full list, visit the Book Industry Study Group website.

## Understanding Your Audience

Imagine that you're preparing a speech for a presentation, and that it's the first presentation of its kind that you'll be doing at this leg of your professional career. You do hours of research and work endlessly to prepare for the big day. And when the morning arrives, you put on the expensive Versace skirt suit you bought especially for the occasion—if you're a woman—your six-inch Christian Louboutin red-bottom heels, get your hair and makeup professionally done, and head to your presentation in a chauffeur-driven Porsche. You are introduced to your audience by a petite woman wearing glasses, and the silence in the small room is broken by muted applause. When you step into the room, you are greeted by the curious, yet slightly uninterested eyes of twenty-six four-year-olds who know they just have to get through this last presentation on "The Danger of Talking to Strangers" and then they'll get to indulge in nap time. But five minutes into your talk they get restless, and one little boy, no...two, now three children raise their tiny hands, asking, all at the same time, if they can go to the bathroom. And just like that, you've lost the attention of the entire room. You blew your presentation. What do you think went wrong? You didn't prepare with your audience in mind.

I cannot stress enough how important it is to know and understand the audience for which you are writing. Understanding, and working to understand, your audience gives you the inside information you need to give them what they want and to deliver your message in a way that will capture their attention. Hence, knowing your audience and writing with them in mind is essential to your success. In the anecdote above, if you understood that you were presenting to four-year-old children, then you'd know that the pomp and circumstance that may thrill a group of elite CEO's in the fashion industry is completely irrelevant to your young listeners. They want to see bright primary colours, animated characterization, and here captivating stories.

Likewise, when writing, say, nonfiction self-help, you have to decide right off the bat whom it is that you are writing for. You may choose to write for young single mothers who feel overwhelmed or maybe business owners over forty who want to take their businesses to the next level. Are you writing religious nonfiction? Then you need to know if you're writing for the churched or the un-churched. Is your audience proficient in the biblical text, exegesis, and hermeneutics? Or is your audience young converts who are still learning how to understand the Bible? It all counts. Whether you're targeting the academic community or the high school drop-out who's trying to start over, it all counts.

Knowing and understanding your audience affects how you write—your word choice, the depth in which you explore the subject, the length of the book, and even how much it costs. When writing for children, it is imperative that you take into account the readership level of your book. Books written for preteens can use larger, multi-syllabic words than books written for toddlers. Hence, you wouldn't write a 200-page paperback book for five-year-olds, devoid of illustrations and pictures, about why it is important to do homework, the same way you wouldn't write a picture book about ponies for philosophy enthusiasts. I'm sure you get the point. Therefore, as you prepare to complete your manuscript, stop and think about whom it is that you'll be marketing this book to and why you think they'll want to read it.

# CHAPTER 3

# Improving Your Writing

W hat's your writing voice? Your writing voice is your own unique style of expressing yourself through literary language. It's how you articulate yourself when writing, how you frame your ideas, how you speak to your audience. It's a mix of personality, talent, and skill.

My writing voice and style have evolved over the years. It was clear that I was a writer by the time I could link words stylistically—by the time I was five years old. I started out writing songs that rhymed in my early childhood, stringing words together that matched rhythmically and appealed lyrically to my childish sentiments. I then graduated to writing poetry in my teen years, while still writing songs. My best friends and I went through a poetry phase that had us sharing the fresh lines of emotions we'd penned each week. Then, as I moved into my undergraduate and post-graduate studies, I fell in love with essay writing, which led naturally to my fascination with articles in my young adult years. Now, still a young adult, I write books. But foundationally, at the base epicentral level, all my writings generate from the same root, the same genetic material—they all have a poetic parentage. It's in me, and I can't seem to escape it. Though nearly everything I write is prose, my natural inclination is to write with the raw emotional, heart-tugging, visual language that is characteristic of poetry. My constant growth and evolution, however, have been beneficial, in that I now write with the advantage of experience. Therefore, I have learned how to be versatile in my writing, when to go deep and when to remain on the shores, by simply changing the sequence of the words I use in a particular context. I now write with my reader in mind.

Developing your own personal style will aid you in improving your writing skills. Never get lost in comparison, trying to write like someone you are not. Every writer has their own idiosyncrasies that can, if executed well, make their audience become enamored with their writing.

Still, it can be a struggle to nail down your own unique voice, especially if you haven't done much writing. However, finding it can usher you into a world of possibility and, dare I say, consistency. You will find that your writing experience is less frustrating and your creative juices are more apt to flow. And the best part is you will likely build a readership that is dedicated to you, simply because they know what to expect when they read your work. It's like going to see a Denzel Washington movie on the sole merit that Denzel Washington plays the starring role. I mean, it can't be a bad movie if he's in it, right?

Here's a quick test that I administer to first-time authors who ask me to help them identify their writing voice. Fill in the blanks below:

1. *If you could describe the way you speak using adjectives, what would they be. List the words that describe the way you speak naturally here:*

_____

_____

_____

_____

_____

_____

_____

_____

2. *List the names of your favourite books.*
   *Why do you like them?*

_____

_____

_____

_____

_____

_____

_____

_____

_____

_____

_____

_____

_____

_____

_____

_____

3. *What kind of person do you imagine reading your book? What are their interests?*

_____

_____

_____

_____

_____

_____

_____

_____

_____

_____

_____

_____

_____

_____

_____

4.  Write about your favourite memory in the lines below, then read it back to yourself aloud. Is there anything that stands out about the way you express yourself?

_____

_____

_____

_____

_____

_____

_____

_____

_____

_____

_____

_____

_____

_____

_____

_____

_____

_____

_____

_____

_____

Chances are you read books that are written in a style that you like. Interestingly, we tend to gravitate to those authors who have similar styles as we do. Also, we tend to imagine our ideal reader the way we imagine ourselves and our writing. Finally, when we are prompted to speak naturally, as in speak about a memory or occurrence, our natural style often bursts through, with little effort. Review your answers above and see if you can identify a pattern as it relates to your style.

Once you've identified a style that matches your natural bent, work on improving it. The more you write and practice writing well, the better your writing will become. The following are a few quick tips to keep handy as you work on completing and improving your manuscript.

# Quick Tips

➢ Be true to your writing voice/style

➢ When in doubt, reread what you've written, aloud. Does your wording make sense?

➢ When it comes to word choice, less is more—less 'big' words, less convolution, and no unnecessary repetition or overstating

➢ Eliminate extra words and the overuse of addictive terms and phrases, for example "very", "so", "you see"

➢ Pay attention to consistency

➢ More of your ideas and less of everyone else's—the reader wants to hear from you, so use less quotes and stay away from over-referencing others, unless it's an academic work

➢ If writing a theologically based book, avoid the impulse to quote the Scriptures in every paragraph. Simply including a reference to the location of the idea or back-up text is sufficient. For example, *"Listen for GOD's voice in everything you do, everywhere you go; he's the one who will keep you on track" can simply be written as (Proverbs 3:6, MSG) in parentheses after the corresponding statement or point*

➢ Don't overuse certain punctuation marks and mechanisms, such as the exclamation mark, rhetorical questions, or words written in all caps. Overuse of mechanisms throughout the text actually diminishes the emphasis intended

➢ Do your research. Research is important, but be balanced in your delivery

➢ Don't give statistics that are based on opinions only, always cite accurate information

➢ Never plagiarize another person's work

# CHAPTER 4

# Developing Your Idea into a Book

N ow that you know the basics as it relates to writing a book as well as improving your skills as a writer, it's time to turn our attention to developing your idea into a book. We all have sparks of genius or moments of breakthrough clarity where we think to ourselves, "I should write a book about that!" But then the idea often gets abandoned a few days later in the graveyard of dead concepts, never again to be heard from, unless of course someone else decides to write a book on the very same thing. And then we pout, because we swear we had the idea first.

Unfortunately, millions of ideas and little sparks of genius have died unrealized because we fail to commit to the process of development. So here are a few steps to utilize when developing your next big idea into a book:

1. Describe your idea?

_____

_____

_____

_____

_____

_____

_____

2. Is the idea viable/marketable?

_____

_____

_____

3. Is it relevant to your community, field, industry, generation, or people group?

_____

_____

_____

4. Do you have enough content to fill up a book?

_____

_____

_____

5. What is the purpose of the book?

_____

_____

_____

_____

_____

_____

_____

_____

_____

_____

6. Who is your audience?

_____

_____

_____

_____

7. Are you qualified to write it?

_____

_____

_____

_____

_____

Now let's break the idea up into smaller parts:

1.  What's the title of the work? What name
    captures your idea best?

_____

_____

_____

2.  What are the main topics that you could
    explore within the scope of this idea?
    Write them here:

_____

_____

_____

_____

_____

_____

_____

_____

3. Let's turn those topics into chapter headings. How many chapters can the book have if you use only the major themes/topics? Write them out in the spaces below:

*Chapter 1:*_____

_____

*Chapter 2:*_____

_____

*Chapter 3:*_____

_____

*Chapter 4:*_____

_____

*Chapter 5:*_____

_____

*Chapter 6:*_____

_____

*Chapter 7:*_____

_____

*Chapter 8:*_____

_____

*Chapter 9:*_____

_____

*Chapter 10:*_____

_____


4. Now let's break it up even more. Use the blank space below to fill in, in point form, the points you'll be discussing in each chapter:

_____

_____

_____

_____

_____

_____

_____

_____

_____

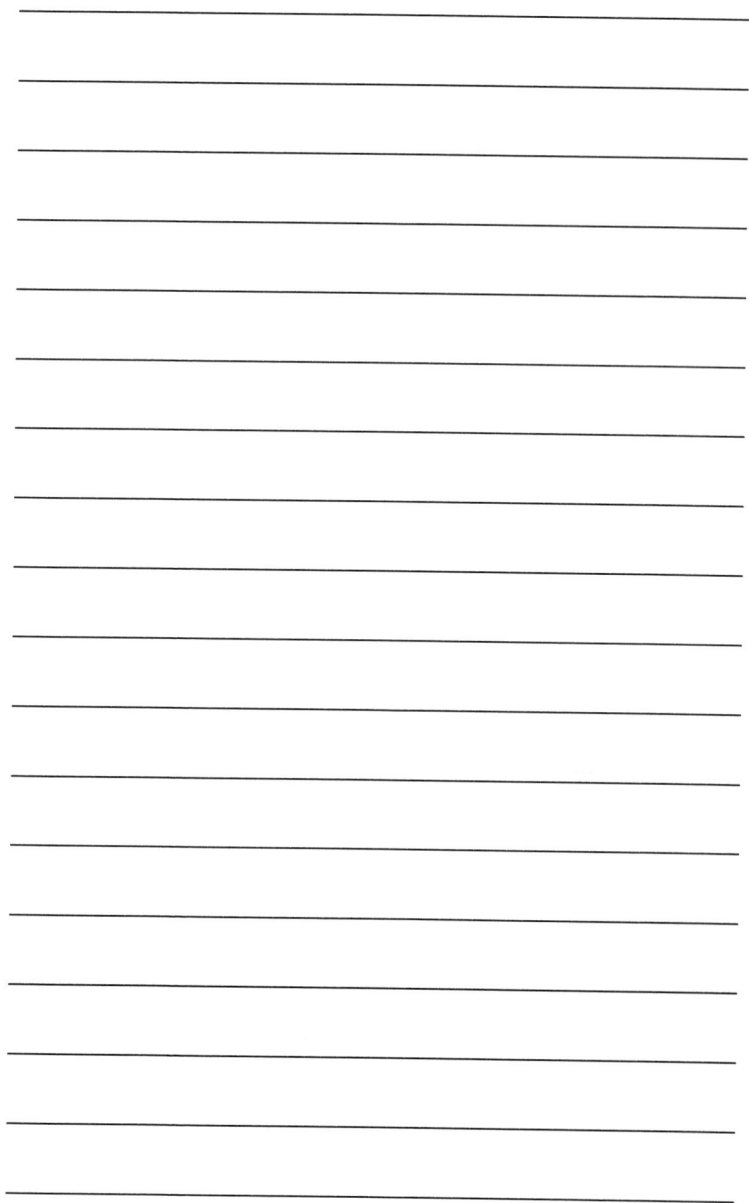

5. Finally, create a writing schedule to help you stay on track. Don't forget to add an introduction to your outline. Can you get the book done in six months? Eight months? A year? Be realistic with your goal. Now write it down and commit to the time allotment you've given yourself.

## My writing schedule is as follows:

*I will complete this book in the next*

_____. *I will do so by writing*

*at least _____ hours per week. My aim is to*

*complete one chapter in _____.*

*I promise myself not to walk away from this idea until*

*I've completed it.*

If you follow the above steps and commit to doing the work it takes, you can weed out the unviable ideas from the ones that are worth pursuing, and complete your manuscript in a specified amount of time. You can do it. I'm cheering for you.

# CHAPTER 5

# Keys to Being a Successful Author

t's a writer's world. As stated before, digital and self-publishing have transformed the ease and speed of which writers can share their message with readers. Amazon quickly proves this fact with the more than 32 million books that it hosts on its global distribution platform. Yet, if you could speak to them, more than half of these authors would tell you that the success they looked forward to experiencing with the release of their books did not pan out the way they expected. That leads me to the five things I'd like to share with you today. There are some key things that all successful authors know, and a few of them are:

## Being a Good Writer Helps

This point may seem obvious to some, but oftentimes people proceed to write a book without actually sitting down and first mastering the art of writing. In fact, not all authors are writers, and not all writers are authors. Avid readers, the ones you want to attract and the ones you want to read your book and review it, can spot a poorly written book as quickly as they can spot a well-written one. If your writing skills need some work, don't be afraid to take a class or two in order to improve. Also, especially if you choose to self-publish, invest in an experienced and skillful editor who can tighten your work and point out any areas that need improvement. And still, a well-written book alone does not guarantee success.

## Be a Reader

Stephen King once said, "If you don't have time to read, you don't have the time (or the tools) to write. Simple as that." This is a truth that is undeniable. Yes, if you're simply making journal entries for an audience of one then there is no need to do any kind of research or indulge in the leisurely reading of educational literature. But if you dare to write more than your private musings and hope to have an audience of more than your closest family members, then taking time to read is essential. What you read is up to you, but I suggest reading a variety of genres and styles, or at the very least exploring, in depth, your topic of interest by reading up on the subject. The more knowledgeable you are as a writer, the higher the probability that you will produce worthy content and be regarded as a voice of influence by others.

## Be Relevant

Ever been the one in the room locked out of the inside joke? I've had that happen to me before, and it didn't feel good. I was seventeen years old, had just moved to a new country, and hadn't yet become acquainted with certain cultural references. I remember sitting in a colourful restaurant one night over a plate of decadent dessert with a cheerful group of newly made friends, struggling to no avail to stay abreast of their cultural lingo and region-specific (inside) jokes. While I was happy to be in the presence of a great bunch of people, my inability to keep up with their conversations made my chuckles forced and me uncomfortable. The night couldn't have ended quickly enough. Now think of writing as a conversation with your audience. Staying current with contemporary social issues gives you access to the important conversations of our time. The more intelligent input you can offer to these dialogues, the more influential your writing becomes. Being relevant comes with understanding your audience and your context. When you know for whom you're writing and the nature of their concerns, you position yourself to write with not only knowledge, but with relevance.

## Be Courageous

The thing about social issues is that they usually facilitate diverse opinions, disagreements, and opposing sides. If you are to add weight to your writing, then you must take a stance. What's your perspective on the issue at hand? Why is it worthy of consideration? When you can answer these questions you arm yourself with content. However, to publish your opinion takes courage, especially if your position is unpopular. Popularity may lead to influence, but so does being willing to go against the grain and speak your truth.

Consider writers like George Orwell, author of the books *1984* and *Animal Farm,* brilliant commentaries on authority and the human condition; or C. S. Lewis, author of *The Chronicles of Narnia*, whose works have influenced the realm of theology, the fantasy genre, and philosophy; or Harper Lee, author of *To Kill a Mockingbird*, whose book tackles racism in America so artistically that it has won multiple awards and has shaped the thinking of many on the topics of race and justice.

It is important to remember that as a writer you

have an inherent ability to be a voice for the voiceless, to shape society's opinions, and to speak to cultural understandings through your art. Influence comes with the ability to fulfill your mandate well and share it with the world through the appropriate channels.

## Know Your Subject Matter, Really Know It

Having expert knowledge on your topic of interest will legitimize your authorship and qualify your voice as an authority on the issue. Research is important. Having a reputation or history of working in that particular field is also important. Writing a book based solely on opinion just isn't good enough, unless, of course, you're writing fiction. And even then, it is still imperative in incorporate some form of research to ensure the accuracy of specific elements in your story. When your audience trusts you, they will buy what you have written.

## Know Your Audience

You'd be surprised how many authors I have encountered who have no clue who their audience is. As a publisher, it is my duty to ask authors who approach me about publishing their book a series of questions, one of which is, "Who is your audience?" If you've never asked yourself this question before, take a moment to think about it. For whom are you writing? And don't say

"Everyone," because not everyone wants to hear what you have to say. You need to know who it is that you're targeting. Is it single women over 30? Teens and young adults? Business professionals? Fitness enthusiasts? Your answer to this will help to direct your writing. Furthermore, knowing your audience also helps you to zero in on what it is that they want to hear and how they want it packaged.

## Utilize Good Promotion and Marketing Techniques

Get used to self-promotion because you're going to have to do lots of it. I know, it can sometimes make you feel queasy just thinking about it. Me too. As a professional who is also an introvert, self-promotion is probably one of my biggest struggles. But it must be overcome in order to share your book with more than your inner circle. You'll have to sell yourself to sell your work. But should all your pep talks to yourself in the mirror fail, there are great marketing consultants who would be more than happy to develop a marketing strategy to help you succeed. Hire one.

Once you've published your book, you'll want to get it into the hands of the influencers in your community. Think media—radio shows, relevant TV shows, newspapers, magazines; think community leaders— motivational speakers, ministers, industry leaders;

think community hubs—libraries, book stores, artist exhibitions. It can seem tiring, especially if you are self-published, but getting great reviews and landing speaking engagements or other mass exposure will bolster your career as an author and push your book further up the ranks of the best-seller list.

## Reform Your Idea of Success

Many first time authors walk into the process of writing and releasing a book with the idea that they will sell thousands of copies and make hundreds of thousands, if not millions, of dollars. Well, that doesn't always happen. If that were true, then every single author on Amazon would be rich. The truth is that releasing a book can result in so much more than money. For example, it can lead to a new career as a sought-after speaker on a particular issue or topic. It can be used as a great promotional tool for the services you offer. It can be used as a professional credit to secure a teaching position at a post-secondary institution. And so much more. The world of a successful writer is complex, and the turnovers are multifaceted. My advice is to approach your career as a writer with an open mind and a flexible will. There will be quiet moments and busy ones. But the world is literally at your fingertips.

# CHAPTER 6

# Writing Your Project Description

O nce you've completed your book, you'll need to promote it in order to increase its probability for success. In order to properly market your book, however, you'll need to know how to describe it in such a way that it grabs the attention of your intended audience, media outlets, and other prime influencers. Using what you've learned throughout this handbook, craft a project description that provides all the pertinent details about your book.

In your description include: the book's genre, length, target audience, its intended purpose, what makes it different from other books in its category, why you are qualified to write it, and why it is relevant to your readers.

Use the space provided to craft a complete professional description of your book.

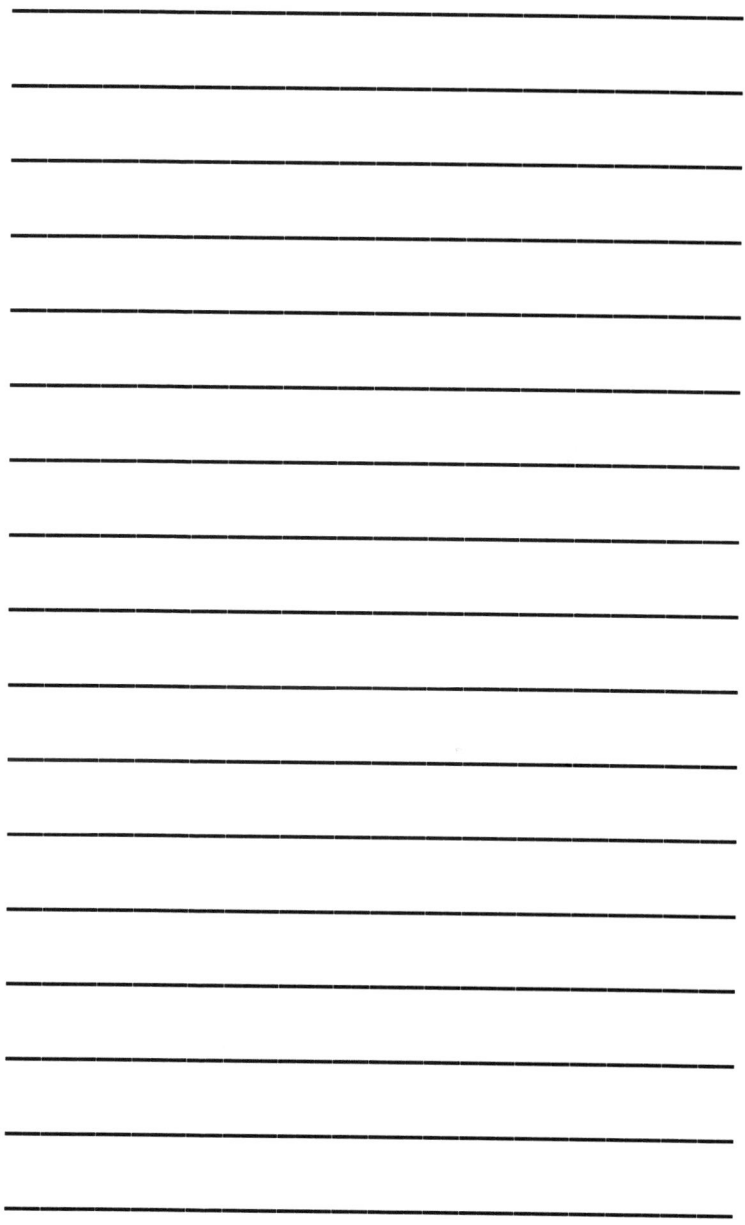

You should now be armed with both a useable outline of your book project as well as a project description that includes all the relevant pieces that industry professionals and community influencers look for.

I trust that you have learned much and that you feel more equipped to move forward in completing your next book. Keep this handbook close by as you embark on your writing journey.

May success be yours.

# Resources

BibleGateway. Biblegateway.*com: A Searchable Online Bible in over 100 Versions and 50 Languages.* Web. 23 Oct. 2015

"Complete BISAC Subject Headings, 2014 Edition." *Complete BISAC Subject Headings, 2014 Edition.* https://www.bisg.org/complete-bisac-subject-headings-2014-edition. 23 Oct. 2015.

Dictionary.com- The World's Favorite Online English Dictionary!" *Dictionary.com.* Web. 23 Oct. 2015.

Printed in Great Britain
by Amazon